EXIT

STRATEGY

GEORGE A. OLOKUN
"Mr-Opportunity"

EXIT STRATEGY

GDot Publishing Group
Atlanta, GA

All necessary written permissions and verbal consents have been obtained for any written work used to support the foundation of this book.

Cover Design by Reginald Bibb
Foreword by Paul Carrick Brunson

Library of Congress Cataloging-in-Publication Data
LCCN: 2014930581

ISBN-13: 978-0615950198
ISBN-10: 0615950191

Printed in USA

First Edition

1 2 3 4 5 6 7 8 9 10

To: Edith

Presented to

3-9-14

Dedication

I dedicate this book to the generation of believers that will pursue and create the life they were born to live!

Be the best you that the World will ever get to meet...

RIP Charles S. Parker (1986-2012)

Acknowledgements

This work is a culmination of research, thoughts, and life experiences that represents the actualization that we can create the life we each desire to live.

All honor, praise and reverence goes to my Lord and Savior Jesus Christ for blessing me with a gift to put words together that can be used to empower others.

I am grateful for each of you that have supported me to this point in my life and I do not take any of you for granted. My path has been all the better because of your many prayers, support, and investments.

—To my mother, father, siblings, and entire family.

—To my close friends and confidants for inspiring me beyond a point that you all will ever know.

—To my mentors for holding me accountable to become the best me I can be.

"Think Strategy"

– Charles S. Parker

RIP 1986-2012

"Meeting with "Mr-Opportunity" to discuss my exit strategy felt more like defining a financial success strategy. Don't let your future become handicapped due to complacency; define your reality by observing what the future can bring. Plan your exit now, or should I say create your future by defining your success."

–Khaleel R. Garcia
Executive Director/Co-Owner
KB Creative Group

"In my time knowing, speaking with, and reading George's books, his words & advice have been guiding principles in the decision-making process for all aspects of my life."

–W. E. W. Russell
Vice President, Systems Integration
incNETWORKS, Inc.

"Most people spend time thinking about change and talking about making a difference, George is a doer and a true catalyst of change."

–Rontavis Shamar Walker
Author, Speaker, Entrepreneur, & Community Leader

"George is an inspiration to this generation and has shown himself to be a global thought leader. I am

confident that he is one of the progressive leaders of this generation and a breath of fresh air to those he come in contact with him."

—Rep. Shevrin D. Jones
Florida House of Representatives
Member, District 101

Contents

Foreword
By: Paul C. Brunson

In this book, George Olokun clearly explains and magnifies a universal EXIT STRATEGY that enables you the reader to adopt an "ALL IN" mindset, resulting in a life paradigm shift and allowing for your individual life purpose to be fulfilled.

When I think back to when George and I met via social media in 2010, it is a prime example of how you never know who is watching what you do and how someone can see what is ahead of you, while you're yet still working towards it. Before the camera's, the bestselling book, the growing global audience and everything that has come to pass over the last 4 years, there was a message from a guy that I had never met in person, nor ever had a full length conversation with. That message was from George and he said to me "there is greatness all over your life, get ready for the doors that are about to be opening to you". Knowing that I was putting in work and eager for what was to come, my response to George was "very strong words bro".

Last year George said to me, your story is a perfect example of the bases of my new book ***Exit Strategy*** and that he wanted me to write the foreword for the new book. **He stipulated that I share my story, and here it is...**

I Never Thought I'd Be Doing What I'm Doing Now...NEVER.

I grew up always thinking I'd be a 'businessman' (funny thing is now I'm a business, man). My early interests were in entrepreneurship and business. My hobbies in high school included writing business plans and reading the Forbes 400 list.

The Moment That Changed My Life

Prior to that point in my life, I had NEVER read a book cover to cover. Scouts honor! I got through all those former English class literature exams, book reports, and homework by skimming. It all changed on a visit to the bookstore, though. While standing in this bookstore, I saw a book awkwardly positioned on the shelf. From a quick glimpse, I was captured by the title "*Why Should White Guys Have All The Fun?*" At the age of 18, it was the first book I purchased for non-academic reasons. Over the next 3 days, I would devour every word of the book, reading it cover to cover twice. I then committed to maintain several of the rituals articulated in the book (like developing life mantras, reading newspapers daily, and most importantly, training my belief system). That one book has had such a profound impact on my life. As a result of the inspiration developed from the book, I shot off in a new life direction like a rocket. I changed every aspect of my life: recommitted spiritually, started eating healthier, exercised with purpose, became a mentor, aggressively pursued my studies, and most importantly, began believing in myself again.

After graduating from college with honors, I entered the professional world as an analyst at an investment bank. At the time, it was my "dream job." I was making 'real' money, had the opportunity to learn from the top financial minds in the world, and did I say I was making money? From the outside, it looked like I was winning! While most of my fellow college grads were taking "any old job" and struggling financially, I was ballin' (ordered my shiny new BMW, copped a Presidential Rolex (well, it was fake but you couldn't tell me otherwise), had an amazing apartment, and first fell in love with European tailored suits). I was living THE life...or so I thought...

.

Two distinct things happened that led me to **exit** the investment banking world:

1) I started getting terrible stomach aches every Sunday night as I prepared for the work week. At the time, I didn't realize it was anxiety. Our bodies are conditioned to inform us when we might not realize what's happening. I listened.

2) A co-worker was praised for not attending his child's birth and instead coming to work for a big project. Yeah, sickening!

A Succession of Business Failures

So, I quit and started a business. Everyone said "Paul you're crazy to quit such a great job." But one of the mantras I had created for myself years earlier was to "always listen to your gut, first." I took my little bit of savings, moved in with Jill's parents (because they lived near the city) and started my first company. That business lasted about 8 months before it collapsed. I then went on to found, run, and subsequently run into the ground three more businesses.

In just 5 years after working at the investment bank, financially the tables had completely turned. No new car, no new clothes, no business, I was broke. However, one thing I always had was my then girlfriend and now wife Jill. She was my rock. Since my 'moment of clarity' in the bookstore at college through the ups and downs, she was by my side. While I had always envisioned being secure in a profession before getting married, I felt I didn't…I couldn't wait any longer.

A few weeks after getting married, I landed a job at Kaplan Test Prep and became the director of one of their 'super' centers. I became the first African American and youngest director for a facility of that size. I loved the work. The team I had was amazing, my bosses were cool, and most importantly, I loved the service side of the job. In particular, I loved that I had full discretion over a tuition assistance program that allowed me to discount (down to a $1) the cost of our tutoring services. While my bosses had no idea, I had nearly all of DC taking courses for $1, especially the High School students I met. There was a certain affinity I had towards the students of public schools in DC. If you read any press about DC public schools, you can see how many of those kids are simply written off. I was so compelled to help them because while in high school I, too, was written off.

A Community Organizer and Service Provider Is Born

Over several years of interacting with schools and volunteering my time after work and over the weekends with various community programs focused on youth, I realized many were missing strong academic resources (materials and instructors). Initially I leveraged my position at Kaplan, but after the demand outstripped my personal supply, I created an idea and wrote a business plan to form a non-profit group to be an "academic engine" for youth programs. I pitched the idea to my bosses for support and got denied. I pitched the idea for support to our competitors, and got denied. I even pitched the idea to local DC government and never got a no, but never got a yes either. Guess that's politics.

The Turk & Me

Around this time of pitching my academic engine idea, I had a chance meeting with a Turkish businessman. The story of our first meeting is so amazing, it deserves its own post but bottom line, it is a perfect example of the power of stepping outside your box. Over casual conversation, with the Turk, he suggested I come to Turkey and pitch the academic engine idea to his team (it so happened that he was the CEO of a large educational holding company).

So not even knowing exactly where Turkey was on the map, I flew to Istanbul and pitched my idea. In what could be a scene out of a movie, seated at a long walnut brown table, with over 24 thick, rich leather chairs surrounding, I shook hands on a deal that would change my life more profoundly than Reginald Lewis' book. Through my newly created deal, I would receive investment to develop my academic non-profit in barter for me working full-time to manage the U.S. academic investments of the firm.

With no contract, just a handshake, I flew back to the States, quit my job and started work in my new career as both the Director of my dream non-profit and the head of U.S. investments for this behemoth international firm...not a bad week!

Over the next several years, I stayed busy. I led the growth of both entities beyond my dreams. On the non-profit side, we served 1000s of low-income students, working with many of the equity holders in the community (schools, volunteer programs, churches, government, and businesses). On the investment firm side, we created one of the largest study abroad programs, a private university, and several dormitory investments (which is actually a very good business). I also had time to squeeze in going to business school at Georgetown and learn to speak Turkish.

A Matchmaker Is Born

By the summer of 2008, I was fully immersed in both of my growing projects and little did I know, 100 DC high school students in a summer camp would change my life, yet again. At the time, my non-profit was managing a program for low income high school students and to kickoff the summer long camp, I went down to work the registration table. As I greeted each student, I asked them basic intake info, with one question being "do your parents live in the household?" After slightly over 100 students enrolled, not one...NOT ONE of the students had two parents in their household. Slightly more than half lived with auntie, grandma, or big sister/ brother the more likely household 'parent.' I could not believe what I witnessed...NOT ONE. Knowing how impactful parents are in the development of a child and to think these 100 would not be blessed with it.

Driving home from camp that day, I couldn't think of anything but those children and what, if anything, I could do. Over dinner that night I discussed what I discovered earlier that day with my wife. We pondered what could be done to help strengthen the nuclear family. Jill and I talked for hours, trading solutions back and forth. We ended the conversation jokingly saying; well maybe we could become matchmakers.

The next morning, I woke up, and with that "matchmaker" comment still on my brain, I started googling everything matchmaker related. Over the next few days, my research continued and I eventually ended up jotting down a list of matchmakers I'd like to call to get further information about the profession. I blocked out a few hours about a week later and started dialing. Out of 10+ calls, not one matchmaker took my call or called me back. I recall one getting back to me via email, offering to schedule a call if I first paid them. WOW! The limited response drove my curiosity even further.

I discovered there was a Matchmaking conference taking place in New York in just a few weeks so I jumped on a train and headed north. My goal at the conference was just to check things out and see what I could learn. What I saw was shocking. There I was in a room with 100+ of the world's top matchmakers and not one of the full-time matchmakers was African-American. Not one of the matchmaker's was under the age of about 40. And I counted only one male matchmaker. Looking around the room is when I had my light bulb moment–there is a seat for me in this industry. I need to become a matchmaker.

How Do You Train To Become A Matchmaker ... Head To Denver!

So, just like when I returned from Turkey years earlier, I came back home from my New York excursion and scheduled a meeting with my Turkish employers to leave my position. And just like leaving the investment bank, just like leaving Kaplan, most of my friends and family said I was crazy to leave such a good job. But this time, they thought I was certifiable. Think about this for a second, I had just graduated from business school, was managing two successful organizations, building an amazing professional network, traveling around the world, and making more money than I ever had...and I wanted to become a matchmaker.

When my mind is committed to something, I'm locked in. So I parted ways with the Turks, converted my non-profit to an all volunteer organization (no longer having the financial support from my friends from across the pond), and dipped into my family's savings. I structured a full year 'matchmaking training program' that would help me best understand the profession. My self-training included studying over 213 books, attending conferences and coaching certifications, pro-bono client practicing, and my capstone was flying to Denver to train under someone I consider to be the best Matchmaker on the planet, Rachel Greenwald.

After 60-70 hours per week of training for a full year, in the winter of 2009, I launched my matchmaking firm! At that moment, I realized I was no longer jumping around my purpose. Becoming a matchmaker and lifestyle coach allowed me for the first time in life to "connect my dots" (as Steve Jobs famously said) and be fully immersed in my purpose from head to toe.

Thinking back now, I see that I implemented an Exit Strategy and worked it till a shift happened.

Paul Carrick Brunson
Best Selling Author, Life Coach, TV Host, & Matchmaker

[*Paul Carrick Brunson & "MrOpportunity" | George Olokun*]

Preface

Growing up I was told that I could become whatever I wanted to become, but in all actuality my path was being created and cultivated for me by my family and my surroundings. When I was in high school I was submerged in an environment that molded my thinking towards a particular career field. One of the only jobs I had while in high school was in a pharmacy.

At that stage of my life I was learning and developing skills that I would later find use of. I was truly passionate about the work I was doing and the impact it had on the lives of those I provided a service to. From my vantage point during that period, nothing in life was more rewarding than putting on a white smock, interacting with patients, making money and filling prescription. All of those things were just puzzle pieces for what would have been progressive failures had I continued to pursue them thinking I was heading in a successful direction.

In 2005, while on my collegiate journey to become a Pharmacist, I realized that though I would be an awesome pharmacist, my purpose was far greater than that. I discovered during that period of my life, that what I once saw as the ultimate level of success was really the furthest thing from success. My limited vision paired with a mindset that had been developed by society and my environment, was my weakness. I was my biggest obstacle, until I found what I was purposed to do with my life and became passionate about that very thing.

This book represents the beginning of a life that each of us can create once we have that moment of clarity, when we realize there must be more to life than the life we are currently living. The implementation of your personal Exit Strategy allows for you to begin feeling the true heartbeat of life. As you read this book imagine that we are having a conversation and let the words have time to digest.

Foundation for your *Exit Strategy*

- Decide that something in your life must change.
- Identify what it is you would rather be doing in life.
- Study those that are successfully doing what you would like to be doing.
- Take time to reflect and visualize yourself doing what it is you love.
- Make your Exit Strategy real to yourself.
- Find an Accountability partner.
- Set a specific deadline for the implementation of your Exit Strategy.
- Write down everything that you want to achieve in the next level of your life.
- ADOPT an ALL-IN MINDSET.
- Implement and Work your Exit Strategy.

Exit Strategy

A means of leaving one's current situation, either after a predetermined objective has been achieved or as a strategy to mitigate failure

"The meaning of life is just to be alive. It is so plain and so obvious and so simple. And yet, everybody rushes around in a great panic as if it were necessary to achieve something beyond them." -*Alan Wilson Watts*

Chapter One

Starting Point

"Your better days are waiting on you to claim them, believe in your greatness and claim ownership of your life" ***-George Olokun***

WHAT WILL IT TAKE FOR YOU TO START DOING WHAT IT IS YOU DESIRE DOING EVERYDAY?

Important Keys to your STARTING POINT

- **Implement a daily routine of including Positive Affirmations of Belief in self**

- **Fall in LOVE with your Ability**

- **Be willing to accept Change**

- **Block out all Negativity**

- **Paralyze your FEAR of FAILURE**

- **Identify a Distraction Free Focus Zone**
    - A place where you are most productive and are able to minimize all outside distractions

- **Become consciously comfortable being uncomfortable!**

I woke up one morning and realized that the life I was living was good, but there had to be something better. The path I was on was fruitful and all roads were leading towards what I perceived success in life to be. My starting point was the moment I began believing in my personal ability and in the talents that I embodied.

Look at life as a never ending learning experience and everything that happens becomes a lesson that better prepares you for the next course.

Understanding Passion and Purpose

Passion and purpose are two things that can operate separately, but are more powerful when consociated. Everyone's purpose has one major commonality and that commonality is rooted in making somebody or something in life better. I discovered my personal purpose was to help others advance in life by understanding the authority they have over their own life.

When you look at life as the adventure it is, there are some amazing things that can come from it. Purpose makes your life come alive and allows you to see a blank canvas of opportunity. That particular opportunity is one that sets itself aside from any other person's opportunity.

The first step to doing something that highlights the reason that you were created on this earth– is to believe and know that you were created to do exactly what you're gifted to do. Meaning you cannot try to do or be something that you weren't created for.

Believe beyond a shadow of a doubt in every aspect of your purpose and through that belief you'll get energy to pursue your passion.

Adopt an **"ALL IN"** mindset, which will result in a paradigm shift and allow you to see the obtainable reality of your purpose being fulfilled. This mindset takes a daily commitment from self to invest all of yourself building everything around your purpose. It is very important that when looking for your passion and your purpose that you start by listening to the very loud, yet silent voice of your mind. Understanding that connecting to the most creative component of your body, that being your mind, will make everything you do make sense to you. Others will make suggestions as to what you should do in life. Many of those suggestions will interest you, but you will quickly reach a glass ceiling if they do not align with your purpose.

There is something special about being around someone that is passionate, but more especially being around someone that knows how to make their passion work for their purpose.

In your journey towards the creation of a new identity around your purpose, there will be times that it seems like life is partaking in a game of hide and seek with your purpose. This is the moment you must find an opportunity to join in the game and search for it. With your paradigm shift around purpose, you will know that you are on the right path because it will seem like you are encountering bumps and having to make a few pit stops. The most important thing to remember is not to get distracted. Living life with a main goal of identifying your purpose and fulfilling it is the true definition of success.

Discovering passion is one of the most rewarding growth moments we have in life. Imagine getting in a car and driving around aimlessly, everywhere you stop becomes your destination and ultimately you're just moving around with time. Finding purpose in life that is magnified by passion, gives every moment of your journey a predetermined destination. You are now free to live life in a space that has no barriers or limitations.

The freedom that passion brings is like a key that opens every lock. When you have a key that opens every lock, everything not only seems possible, but proves to be possible. Fear, doubt, insecurities, and other obstacles are erased from your life's equation. Passion paves a road so that purpose can travel into uncharted territory. Only then can you expect to feel the true heartbeat of life and see your life come alive.

Your exit strategy will only gain real momentum when it becomes real to you. If you try to hold on to the fear of the unknown, you will cause your exit strategy to fail in its early stages.

BUCKLE UP,

ENJOY THE RIDE,

FORECLOSE ON FEAR AND FAILURE!

NOTES

NOTES

"The conceptual reality of creating the life you desire to live, instead of remaining in a place in life of merely existing, is the lighted path for those that decide to make a conscious detour, in a more progressive direction for their life journey."

–George Olokun

Chapter Two

Living-Vs-Existing

"Just because you are breathing doesn't mean you are alive" ***-Unknown***

WHY WERE YOU CREATED?

Six questions to see if you are Living-Vs-Existing

- Are you fulfilled with your current life?

- Do you make time to appreciate the simple things in life?

- Does your inner happiness align with your outward display of happiness?

- Do others identify you with what you are passionate about?

- Do you wake up excited about embarking on your day and all that it will bring?

- Can you clearly express what it is you were created to do in life?

From the moment you take your first breath, there is a clear indication of your existence. Existence is a gift that we are all afforded during the allotment of time we have here on earth.

For centuries there have been several studies on existence or "Ontology" as it is formally defined– *the metaphysical science or study of being.* Many in western philosophy treat metaphysics as the study of "higher" reality or "invisible" nature of everything. Parmenides of Elea, an ancient Greek philosopher, is attributed with influencing the whole history of western philosophy and is often seen as its grandfather.

When you think about life and the reality of life, the redundant connectivity between existence and active living are reliant on each other. For example, in order for you to decide to live rather than just exist, you must first experience how mundane life is when you are just existing and going with the passing of time. It is very easy for you to confuse existing with living, because often enough you are busy with life and you're attaining things you feel are validating your life.

Step One to Living vs. Existing: *Get Focused*

Society would have you believe that being "BUSY" constitutes a life well lived, but that is the furthest thing from truth. Most of the time when someone is busy, they really couldn't articulate what came of their busyness. There are several things that you can do to determine whether there's substance to your busyness or not.

For starters, get yourself a notebook or mobile application that you can use to organize your daily, weekly, and monthly priorities.

Categorize the items of your life in three areas—***mandatory for survival, elective tasks, and miscellaneous***. By doing this simple task you will free up a lot of time you currently spend doing any and everything put in front of you.

Area 1: *Mandatory for survival*

These are things that you have committed to doing and that are interdependent with you, such as going to work, bills that must be paid, taking care of family needs, etc...

Area 2: *Elective tasks*

These are tasks that often make up a large percentage of your busyness. They could be classified as mandatory but are indeed elective, because if they don't get done by you the world will not come to a crashing halt.

Area 3: *Miscellaneous*

These are task that you have no knowledge of until they are placed on your lap. Usually these tasks are urgent to someone else as a result of their lack of planning. Do not allow your time to be overly consumed by these tasks.

Step Two to Living vs. Existing: ***Slow Down***

The findings of a survey entitled *Life in the Fast Lane*, highlights that adults aged 25 and over are struggling to juggle work commitments with the demands of family and keeping up with friends. *One in five adults admits to taking work home to finish over the weekend, while half of all respondents reported feeling stressed on the weekend at least once a month.*

The 'fast-lane' approach to living means 61 percent of adults spend only between 15 and 30 minutes eating their evening meal. Impatience and anxiety or a wish to avoid even the slightest delay appeared to be symptomatic of fast-lane living.

More than half of respondents admitted to passing through traffic lights on red, while 58 percent use their car for short journeys rather than walk.

Almost three-quarters said they would put the phone down rather than wait on hold, while 84 percent admitted to saving a few seconds by walking on moving escalators.

Nearly six out of ten people said they felt they were 'missing out' on something but did not know what.

How often have you asked yourself— *What was I created to do?* I guarantee that you are not the only one that has had these words race up and down the active crevasses of your mind. Once you take the necessary time to slow down and answer that question, you will begin the journey towards actually living verses just existing.

Step Three to Living vs. Existing: *Believe*

Whenever you hear the word believe you probably think of this invisible agreement to something you cannot see or touch. Belief is actually the psychological state in which an individual holds a conjecture or premise to be true. Establish a belief in yourself and make it so solid that you believe that there is no limit to what you are capable of achieving.

Follow these six rules when building the foundation for living.

Rule #1:

Trust yourself.

Rule #2:

Operate outside the limitations set by others.

Rule #3:

Eliminate the concept of failure.

Rule #4:

Block out all naysayers.

Rule #5:

Surround yourself around others that are "living" and not just existing.

Rule #6:

Spend time focusing on your inner peace and on obtaining maximum fulfillment.

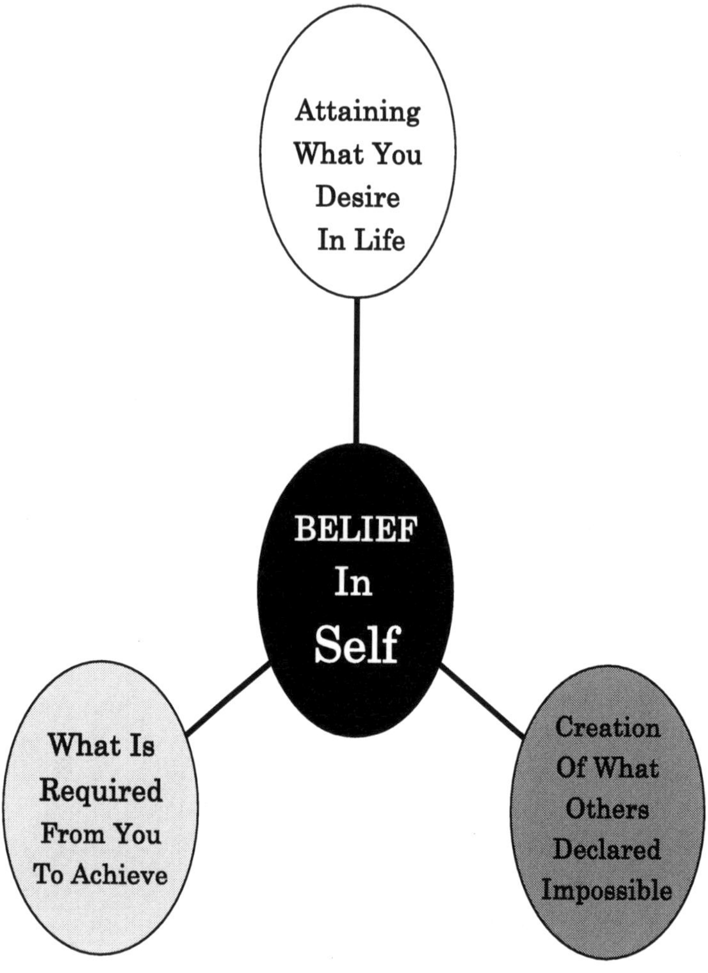
Attaining What You Desire In Life
BELIEF In Self
What Is Required From You To Achieve
Creation Of What Others Declared Impossible

NOTES

NOTES

Chapter Three

Nighttime Entertainment

"A dream that isn't turned into a vision and then turned from a vision into action, is merely nighttime entertainment" ***-G. Olokun & J. Bland***

ARE YOU READY TO STOP DREAMING ABOUT WHAT YOU DESIRE?

- What good is your dream if it only remains housed in the repositories of your mind?

- Understand that there is a clear difference between a dream and a vision.

- Do not invest mental work hours creating something you do not plan to invest physical hours to create.

- When you write down your thoughts you are more likely to make them come to life.

- Live in your NOW!

- Disconnect from unrealistic ambition and connect with the realistic creation of your reality.

Throughout the duration of your life and possibly even while you slept last night; you experienced something known as a dream. It is even possible that you experienced several dreams, one after another. Studies have shown that the content and purpose of dreams are not definitively understood. Scientist have gathered that the average person has between three to five dreams per night and that each dream can last from a few seconds, to as long as twenty minutes.

One of the world's most renowned thought leaders Deepak Chopra, posed a question in his thought module entitled Chopra Well– that question being *"Are You Living In A Dream World?"* He clearly explained that a dream world is a mental world completely and totally. Deepak went on to explain that a person's perception reality is not reality; it's a projection of their internal dialogue.

I can personally attest to having had some nighttime dream experiences that were very entertaining and even some dreams within dreams. The result of all of those dreams, were that they did not manifest into anything outside of entertainment. Despite how real the dreams felt, I have nothing to show for those dreams.

To take it a step further, I remember the day I woke up from the cycle of living in a dream. We all have heard this sayings–►►► **DREAM BIG**, but if you are dreaming you are not wake.

Day Dreaming

If you would be honest with yourself you would admit that sometimes you spend a great deal of time day dreaming about places you would like to go, people you would like to have around or be similar to, and things that you hope to one day acquire. But if you spend all of your time day dreaming, when will you have the time to get closer to those things you desire? You would not go to work ten hours a day, five days a week and be ok with not receiving some sort of payment for the work you have done, **would you**? Then why would spend mental work hours thinking about and replaying a dream in your mind without being able to see some tangible results for all the mental work hours you have invested?

Is it possible to dream while you are awake? The answer is **NO**!

One of the reasons you have not been able to grab a hold of what it is you desire from your life, is that you are being entertained by the idea of what you desire. Dreams are a form of idea and that idea must be transformed into a vision. Once the dream is a vision, the vision must then become a plan and once it is a plan you have to then turn it into your present reality.

Have you heard of Life Centered Present Moment Awareness?

> Deepak describes it as the art of separating the moment from the situation surrounding the moment. *"When you are awake you see yourself as the creator of your own life; the author of your own life, you go beyond a more trans-present self."*

As a part of your exit strategy you must commit to maximizing on the time you spend in the present moment. Every dream you have will not become the new reality for your life. Strategically select which dreams you are willing to invest both metal and physical work in, ultimately enabling yourself to live the best life you desire to live. Once you have decided to invest in the said dream or idea, follow these five steps to ensure the success of your strategy.

Step 1: *Open Your Eyes*

When you open your eyes and focus on your dream, you then turn that dream into you **present moment vision.** A present moment vision is the experience of seeing something in the now that is yet to be physically created. This makes the dream real to you, even though others that might get wind of your dream might not see what you see.

Step 2: *Write Down Details*

Writing is a form of art and by writing your vision, you begin to create what could become a masterpiece. For every vision you write down, it's as if you are paying your mind for the mental work hours it has spent to create that vision. It is in this step that you kill off the initial attack of doubt, fear, and anything else that would try to obstruct your sight around this present moment vision.

Step 3: *Establish Timelines and Expiration Dates*

Time is one thing that moves with or without you. In order to use time effectively and to be efficient you must identify the timeline for your vision and create an expiration date for the implementation of that timeline. It's very important to understand that the timeline is something that will vary per the person and per the vision. For there to be an expiration date established you must determine the starting point of your timeline. Once you have established your starting point, you should not exceed a period of twenty-four months before implementing your timeline.

> *Example:* If my vision is to become a personal trainer, from the moment I make that decision, the time clock is ticking. This doesn't mean that I will be a personal trainer in twenty-four months; it means that I should not still be merely thinking about becoming a personal trainer, but that I must begin putting in physical work hours towards that vision.

The expiration date of my thought process should fuel action towards my timeline. Though it may take another twenty-four months of physical action before I acquire the necessary training, knowledge, and skill needed to be a personal trainer, my timeline will account for that before I set out on the journey.

Step 4: *Fully Commit To Yourself*

You are one of the most important people, if not the most important person that your future is reliant upon. Do not try to rush the journey of life, because all you would be doing is cheating on yourself. Stay committed to achieving what you set out to achieve. Things will happen along the way to acquiring the things you desire for your life.

Step 5: *Experience The Experience*

Take the necessary time to soak up every life moment, every memory, and every challenge that comes from the experience known as life. I encourage you to keep a journal and make notes about how you overcome the challenges that are birthed as a result of your vision being birthed, as a reminder that it was all a part of the journey experience.

NOTES

NOTES

Chapter Four

Reflection in Life's Mirror

"If today was the last day of my life, would I want to do what I am about to do" **-Steve Jobs**

WHO DO YOU SEE WHEN YOU SEE YOURSELF?

- Is your life image aligning with the image of the life you desire?

- Take control of what reflections your life will produce.

- When you live trying to be who others envision you to be, you rob yourself of that signature identity the world needs.

Who is it that you see when you look into life's mirror? —*better yet*, who do others see when they look into the mirror that houses your reflection? It is amazing how most live life making sure that the image being reflected —*their image*, is one that makes others happy, but do not focus on the happiness of the person that is being reflected.

Our mental images of ourselves help determine how we react to daily highs and lows of life. If we think of ourselves as worthwhile and valued, that quality will come across to other people. Molded by both internal and external forces, our self-image makes a huge difference in how we feel and act.

A recent poll conducted by the American Psychological Association found that one-third of Americans are extremely stressed out. Finances and work were the top stressors, leading to increased health problems, bad relationships and reduced productivity. Forty-one percent of people under such high levels of stress recognized a negative impact on their self-image.

Over the past 7 years, I conducted a field study on different types of images that are reflected in the mirror of life. What I concluded was that there are three general reflections that we can all identify with.

These reflections are:

1. **Personal Mental Image**
2. **Personal Public Image**
3. **Actual Reflective Image**

Image One: ***Personal Mental Image***

This image is a reflection of who you see in your mind. It holds so much weight when it comes to determining what you aspire to become and what you are willing to do to make this image the reality of your life. Sadly most never get to lay eyes on this image in real life, because they are actually afraid of it. Afraid because it requires them to step away from the comfortable image they have programmed as their primary image.

Image Two: Personal ***Public Image***

Public image is the image that seems to enslave people. People make judgments about other people based on three elements. How you dress, how you speak and how you act. We tend to put a lot of time focusing on this image, because on every front we are told how important it is. Your personal can image affects your success in society, your personal life and your public life. Once you get passed the visuals, you begin to learn about the person. Things like personality, values and judgment is also part of personal public image. Personal public image includes self esteem, values, character, personality and much more.

Image Three: ***Actual Reflective Image***

This image here is the real deal. It is the outward reflection that cannot be denied. Your actual reflective image is the natural unenhanced reflection that we try our hardest not to identify with in most cases. This image causes you look at yourself and see the actual flaws you posses that you don't see in your mind.

You must free yourself of the stress and false reality that your reflection can sometimes present. When you are living the life you desire to live, doing the things that you are passionate about and that you are purposed to do, will help you create one image that combines all three of those images. The new image will become your new reality and you must own it.

NOTES

NOTES

Chapter Five

Prisoner of Stability

"Remembering that you are going to die is the best way to avoid the trap of thinking you have something to lose" ***-Steve Jobs***

WHEN WILL YOU BREAK THE CHAINS THAT YOU HAVE BECOME COMFORTABLE WEARING?

Waking up daily to continue living in a cycle consisting of going to a job that you hate, being outwardly happy and inwardly unfulfilled, and acquiring things to impress people that do not really care for you– only highlights the reality that you are a prisoner of stability and that you are not really living the life you were created to live. Stability is defined as a property of body that causes it when disturbed from a condition of equilibrium or steady motion to develop forces or moments that restore the original condition.

Prisoners are people who are deprived of their liberties against their will. The earliest evidence of the existence of the prisoner dates back to 8,000 BC in Lower Egypt. Another way to describe a prisoner is someone that is enslaved.

One thing that some find comfort in as prisoners is the idea of stability. Prisoners become complacent because they know they are guaranteed a place to sleep, three consecutive meals, some clean wardrobe, and a means to stay clean. When I was growing up, I always feared the idea of becoming a prisoner. As I began to look at what path to follow, I made the conscious effort to select the most stable of paths. There was a problem with that effort. The problem was that the stability I was longing for was just another form of enslavement. On that path, the money would be great, but I would have been a prisoner. My days would be controlled by someone or something else and I would be trapped, feeling as if I had to maintain a certain lifestyle that came with that career path. Finding the key that unlocked the chains of stability and it freed me from the prison sentence. That key was a shift in the way I approached life.

Generations of very gifted people have lived their lives under the prison sentence of stability. It's as if around a very young age, they were snatched of their liberties, their ambition, and their freedom to create whatever amazing thing their mind could challenge them to create. All of that freedom was replaced with this dream of having the best house, best car, best wardrobe, and the best of everything that can be bought. Don't confuse what I am saying, those things are all enjoyable to have and there is nothing wrong with having the best of what life has to offer, it is all about what you are chasing. Those generations of people have cheated themselves out of experiencing life in its most natural and creative forms. One of the wealthiest places on earth is the graveyard, because there are so many that have died without ever allowing the value of the gift they were given to share with the world, to come out of them.

The day I freed myself from being a prisoner of stability was the day that I reconnected with life. A one on one conversation with self, helped me to realize that my number one priority was to be the best me that I was created to be. In order for that to occur I had to spend the necessary time getting to know myself. **GET TO KNOW YOURSELF!** Learning what I was passionate about, what my gift was, and understanding my purpose here on earth, all contributed to my freedom. The clarity that came from that conversation with self was that I had to redefine what I saw as "success". When my life focus changed, the direction of my life changed.

Get To Know Yourself

Start having one-on-one conversations with self. These conversations should always begin with you listening to your thoughts and you determining what the topic of that personal dialogue needs to be.

Six Questions to ask self

1. **Mind, what are you trying to tell me about my life?**

2. **Am I tired of being a prisoner to this thing known as stability?**

3. **What sacrifices will I need to make?**

4. **What do I need to do to let the value of my gift be present to me and others?**

5. **How would I feel if I am in the same place I am in now, next year?**

6. **Do I have commitment issues?**

This dialogue should serve as the beginning of many regular self conversations. The beauty of your past life experiences, is the positive or negative residue that you can use as references when making decisions with self.

NOTES

NOTES

Chapter Six

Decisions Decisions Decisions

"We choose not to choose when we have too many options" -Unknown

WHAT WILL IT TAKE FOR YOU TO DECIDE TO DO WHAT YOU DESIRE IN LIFE?

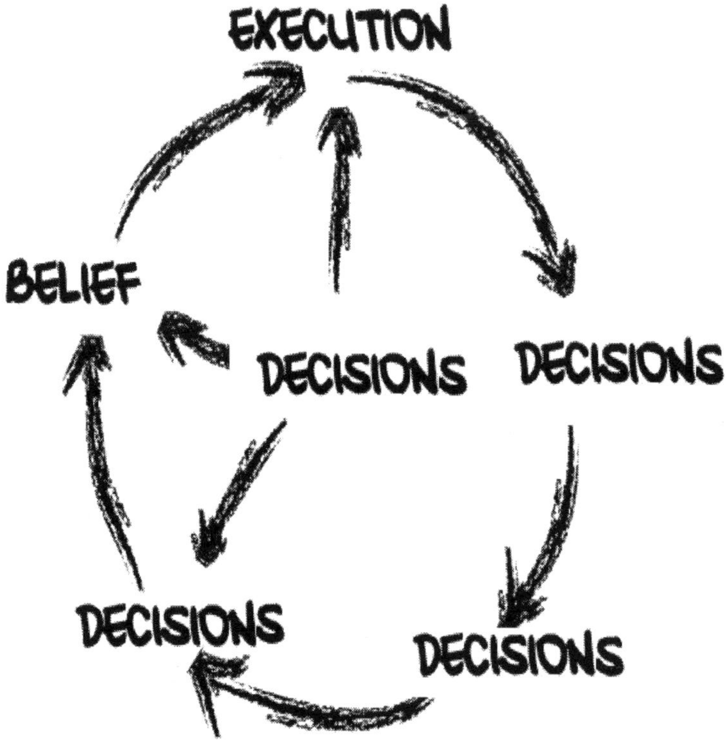

Decisions bring about more decision! Belief in and the Execution of those decisions are important in the decision making cycle.

Life is a four letter word that carries the weight of every decision that you make. Let's face it, how many times have you asked yourself *WHY? —Why are there so many decision that we have to make each day in life?*

What should I eat?
Where will I live?
Who should I date?
Who should I befriend?
What church will I join?
Where will I work?
What kind of automobile should I buy?
What type of toothpaste will I use?

Decisions are the fabric that makes us who we are in life and are critical to our freedom and well being.

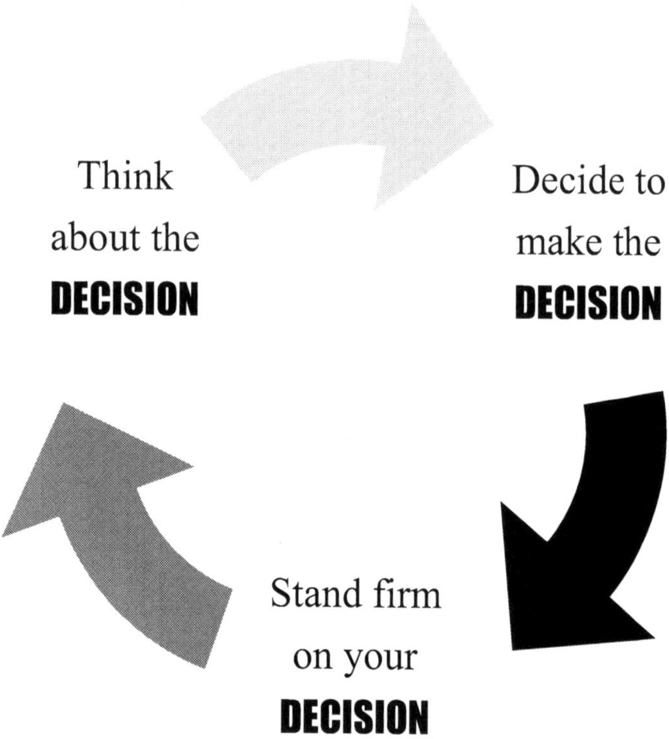

Which way you go in life can determine if your life is stressful, happy, sad, or fulfilling. The best decision you will ever make is the decision to leave your current place in life, to pursue one that makes you come alive. That moment is very liberating and brings much clarity to your life.

A close friend of mine, Brandon Okpalobi, shared his exit strategy from Corporate America with me and though the decisions he had to make were tough, they changed the reason he now wakes up every morning.

Brandon's Story

Brandon once asked me– *Do you know what really grinds my gears?* Before I could respond he replied– *Bureaucracy– it is the exact reason why I am no longer in Corporate America.*

At his last Corporate America job he had a very incompetent supervisor, as I am sure you can probably agree with him if you are currently working in Corporate America. He once asked about the company's plans for professional development and opportunities for growth. He said his boss literally said, "I never thought of that."

Brandon's Life Changing Decision

The day that his supervisor voiced to him that he had no plans regarding professional development or growth in the company for his staff, is the day he made the decision in his mind to quit. Brandon did not walk out the door at that moment, but mentally he had checked out. His performance headed into a downward spiral, to the point that he did as little as necessary to meet minimum requirements.

He decided that he didn't need them when he had himself. That day was the birth of Brandon's passion venture, DIBIA Athletic Development.

> *"I had a vision, believed in myself, conquered my fears, and became an entrepreneur."*
>
> *–Brandon Okpalobi*

So many things frustrated him so he decided to find solace in the things he loved like athletics and clarity came in those moments. Then he realized that for the money he was making he could make the same amount and eventually more by putting his efforts toward something he was truly passionate about and for which he had a vision.

Miami, Florida, October 17, 2011 would be the day he would start jotting down ideas for the DIBIA TAKEOVER and the day that his exit strategy was created.

Brandon Goes All In

Brandon told me he remembers writing almost 100 bullet points on how to make his company successful. One of his early challenges was that he couldn't figure out a name for his business until, he randomly looked at his middle name on a document, *"AzukaDibia"* which together means "your back is stronger than the witch doctors magic." When you separate the two, DIBIA by itself stands "Master of wisdom or knowledge." That's when the light bulb in his head went off.

From there he researched the best organizations in his area of business and then started laying the groundwork for DIBIA Athletic Development.

The 1270 contacts in his phone were the first group that he reached out to, because he believed that any and every person could be of assistance to him in his new venture. Brandon realized and noted that -*when you become an entrepreneur you have to be ready for the people who won't help you because you started your "little business" and the naysayers will not see your perceived future of success.*

Mission Accomplished

His company's mission was to promote excellence in the global community through life skills and enrichment sports programs. He started a Life Skills Program called **D.R.E.A.M.**

DEVELOPMENT THROUGH
RECREATIONAL
EDUCATION FOR
ATHLETIC
MINDS

D.R.E.A.M. is DIBIA Athletic Development's global community outreach initiative that focuses on an athlete's motivational foundation by bridging together excellence, leadership, training and good sportsmanship. Believing "Life Is Filled with Opportunities, Not Entitlements", the D.R.E.A.M. initiative educates athletes on essential core value systems, allowing for the development of a well-defined blueprint for success and cultivation of good stewards of the community.

Through giving back and showing athletes that there are more ways to play a role in sports than just being a physical athlete we will empower them to achieve greatness.

The next step in establishing your personal exit strategy must involve some decisions that ultimately make you uncomfortable— whether it is you leaving the current job you are on or ending the relationship that you are in.

- If some life decisions don't make you somewhat uncomfortable, then you are not making the right kind of decisions.

- Decisions should come with an overall sacrifice of something.

- When you are faced with as difficult decision, go with the decision that yields the long-term return.

NOTES

NOTES

Chapter Seven

Heartbeat of Life

"Control is the inner disease of those who need stability and order to function."
—Mary E. DeMuth

WHAT MAKES YOUR HEART BEAT?

When you think about your life, what feelings do you experience? Is it stress, excitement, fulfillment, depression, heartache, determination, peace, hatred, love, and or do you unsure of that feeling? What is it that wakes you up in the morning? What do you go to bed thinking about at night? I hope you took the time to allow yourself to come up with answers to those questions. Sometimes the feelings from our experience with life are extremely positive and refreshing, but sometimes it's the complete opposite. How you live life is an instrumental piece to how you will experience it.

Think back to your fifth birthday, did you have a birthday cake? Try to remember what it was that you wished for when you blew out the candles on your cake. Some will be able to remember that far back and even remember the cake and even see the image of them blowing out the candles, but that might just be all they are able to or want to remember. Others won't want to remember that moment in life because of what that period in their life represents to them.

Whether your childhood was filled with joyous memories, or if your childhood was a horrible memory that you have attempted to bury deep down in the repositories of your mind, those life experiences happened and cannot be altered. The realization that life moments and life experiences cannot be altered after they occur, makes you live creating moments that you would want to relive over and over again.

Place your hand on the right side of your throat, now place two fingers firmly on the veins in your left wrist, and finally place your right hand over the center of your chest. You might be wondering why I had you to perform those tasks and if you actually followed my directions, more than likely you have already figured it out. The common results of that task should be consistent across the board, if there is blood flowing through your body as it should be. A heartbeat should have been felt at all three of those points. Every time you feel, it represents one complete pulsation of the heart. The heart is one of the most important functioning organs that we as humans need to remain alive.

What in your life represents your heart? To help you answer that question, I would tell you that your career represents your heart because without it there is nothing driving your life's existence. Humans spend an average of 2,628 hours working per year. In a year there are 8,760 hours. Of those 8,760 hours we sleep about 2,920 hours, which leaves 3,212 hours once you subtract sleep and work from the equation. This information goes against the mindset many have when they say there is no time to live. Honestly, when you begin to align the things in your life, you will learn how spend around 8,760 of those hours living life. ***How is this possible you ask?*** Well...

- When your job becomes a way of life and not just a paycheck, you align a major component of your life and your time.

- Adding activities that increase your excitement levels, help you align another major component of your life and your time.

- Erasing the things that affect your personal mood in a not so positive way, helps you to regain control of a large percentage of your time.

- Creating positive affirmation circles helps to give life an added value that helps you and others, which also helps to align your life and makes life all the more worth living.

- Change the type of people that you decide to keep around, replace people that are dull and dry, with people that squeeze as much from life as life has to offer.

NOTES

NOTES

NOTES

Chapter Eight

All In

"No matter how bad it is or how bad it gets, I AM GOING TO MAKE IT!" **-Les Brown**

HOW BAD DO YOU WANT IT?

- Write down why it is important for you to make it.
- Decide what you must sacrifice to achieve the life you desire.
- Commit to sacrificing the necessary things and stick to your commitment.
- Delete your Plan B or your "Backup plan".
- Find your area of balance.
- Accept the fact that things will get tough and that you will make it past the tough times.

One day I was watching a speech given by a notable speaker and that speaker began his speech with the story about the Chinese bamboo tree. He started by saying— *I like the story of the Chinese bamboo tree: You take a little seed, plant it, water it, and fertilize it for a whole year, and nothing happens. The second year you water it and fertilize it and nothing happens. The third year you water it and fertilize it and nothing happens. How discouraging this becomes! The fifth year you continue to water and fertilize the seed and then---take note. Sometime during the fifth year, the Chinese bamboo tree sprouts and grows* ***NINETY FEET IN SIX WEEKS****!*

After hearing this story I had to go research how true it was and I discovered that it was indeed a true story. In my research I also discovered that in order for the bamboo tree to have a successful growth process, that over the five years it takes for it to grow, its daily regimen of watering, general nurturing, and Mother Nature's various contributions had to be consistent, to the point that if that regimen was altered, the bamboo tree would not grow.

Several years ago, *2008 to be exact*, a good friend of mine decided to adopt an all in mindset. He made the decision that he would live his life as if his dreams were inevitable. He packed everything he could fit in two suitcases and caught a one-way flight to Los Angeles. His mission: create art, make a living, feel alive, and in some way impact the world.

He had unknowingly created an exit strategy, which he would only begin to know as his journey. This friends name is *James R. Bland*, a Florida native that decided to go all-in. As he so eloquently put it, *"I'm figuring it all out as I go. I'm grateful for the path I've chosen and I'm optimistic about the future. I know the best is still yet to come and I honestly believe that what God has for me is greater than anything my imagination can conceive."*

James would often say that nothing was promised to him in LA except that in which God had placed in him. There was no tangible promise, but he had a vision and believed that God was going to provide. He went all in and trusted him and trusted the possibility of what could be. Rough times came even after he made it to LA to pursue what he knew was his passion. He rode the bus for 6 months, walked many miles, was robbed at gun point, slept on a few couches — all in the pursuit of fulfilling that burning desire within to create the life he desired.

How Bad Do You Want It?

Are you so fed up with your current life situation that you have that itching desire to do something else? It is not until you get to that point when you can truly say you are ready for an exit strategy. I caution you not to prematurely get to a point the "sound good". The "sound good" is exactly that, doing something because it sounds good. If that is why you try to implement an exit strategy you have a high chance of failing.

The All-in mindset requires that you erase your plan b and focus all your attention, all of your time, and all or your resources on your "plan only".

Alan Watts gave a speech entitled "What would you do if money were no object". This speech is truly interwoven with why an exit strategy is even warranted and why when you adopt this All-In mindset you are able to accomplish more in your life.

Here is his speech:

> *What do you desire?*
>
> *What makes you itch? What sort of a situation would you like?*
>
> *Let's suppose – I do this often in vocational guidance of students. They come to me and say, "Well, uh, we're getting out of college, and we haven't the faintest idea of what we want to do."*
>
> *So I always ask the question,* ***"What would you like to do if money were no object? How would you*** **really** ***enjoy spending your life?"***
>
> *Well, it's so amazing. As a result of our kind of educational system, crowds of students say, "Well, we'd like to be painters, we'd like to be poets, we'd like to be writers. But as everybody knows you can't earn any money that way."*
>
> *Or another person says, "I'd like to live an out-of-doors life and ride horses."*
>
> *I said, "Do you want to teach at a riding school? Let's go through with it. What* do *you want to do?"*
>
> ***When we finally got down to something which the individual says***

he really wants to do. I will say to him, "you do that, and forget the money.

Because ***if you say that getting the money is the most important thing, you will spend your life completely wasting your time. You will be doing things you don't like doing in order to go on living that is to go on doing things you don't like doing.***

Which is STUPID!

Better to have a short life that is full of what you like doing than a long life spent in a miserable way.

And after all, if you do really like what you're doing, it doesn't matter what it is, you can eventually become a master of it. It's the only way to become a master of something, to be really with it. And then you'll be able to get a good fee for whatever it is.

So don't worry too much. Somebody's interested in everything. And anything you can be interested in, you'll find others who are.

But it's absolutely stupid to spend your time doing things you don't like in order to go on doing things you don't like and to teach your children to follow in the

same track. *See, what we're doing is we're bringing up children, and educating them to live the same sort of lives we're living in order that they may justify themselves and find satisfaction in life by bringing up* their *children to bring up* their *children to do the same thing. It's all wretch and no vomit. It never gets there!*

And so therefore it's so *important to consider this question.* ***"What do I desire?"***

NOTES

NOTES

Chapter Nine

Expiration Date

"Your time is limited, so don't waste it living someone else life" ***-Steve Jobs***

EVERY SUCCESSFUL EXIT STRATEGY BEGINS WITH PRESDETERMINED DEADLINES!

- 24 months should be the maximum time allotted from an effective exit strategy.
- Every moment in your exit strategy must be accounted for and you should not base your timeline on the timeline of others.
- Start from the expiration date you set and work backwards when establishing tangible milestones and your desired deliverables.
- You must be able to visualize yourself in every step of your timeline.
- Do not wait until you are almost to your preset expiration date before you begin gauging your progress.

Most if not all of the items produced as a means to add value to our well being come to us with a label identifying that product. On that label one will find a number of things, including where that product was created or shipped from, what the contents of that product are, but the most important thing to us is usually the series of numbers that are printed somewhere on that label. Those numbers are widely identified as the shelf life or the expiration date. It is deemed an important value to the label because it's the length of time that q commodity can be stored without becoming unfit for use.

Your life has an expiration date and that date is unknown to you. The things that you desire to achieve in life have expiration dates as well and when you become the creator of your life, you are able to set those dates. When you are deciding to implement an exit strategy from your current state in life, an expiration date is MANDATORY! This particular expiration date should not exceed a 24 month time period. Think about it like this— imagine you get into your automobile and you just begin to drive with no predetermined destination in sight. Every stop along the way becomes your destination and there will be no way to gauge if you have reached where you desired to be, because you didn't start your journey with a predetermined destination in sight.

Why would you continue living life without a predetermined destination? Your expiration date is the way you gauge your progress while you are on the path towards your desired life destination. It should serve as your constant reminder to stay on track and help you to structure your exit strategy.

Close your eyes and envision where you hope to one day end up. Think about the specific details of your surroundings of that place you desire to one day be. Do you have that vision in your mind? Is it clear? Can you see the specific details in that image? That image is symbolic of the product produced post your expiration date. It represents the end of your journey and the moment when what you envision becomes your present reality.

On every timeline there is an endpoint, that endpoint is decided before the timeline even begins. Your greatest "frenemy" is time; on one side time can pass you by and on the other side time can keep you on track. Time holds you accountable to the things you speak that you want for your life.

Every sports game, church service, workday, concert, and anything that we engage in as humans are all allocated a set amount of time.

Literally, when you look at life in slow motion and begin to pay closer attention to details, you find out that things are given time limits because there's only so much time that we can tolerate certain things with our attention spans. Our attention span is the amount of concentrated time on a task without becoming distracted. Psychologists agree that the ability to focus attention on a task is crucial for the achievement of one's agenda.

Sustained Attention

Most humans are unable to sustain attention on one thing for a long period of time. While sustain attention is the level of attention that produces consistent results on a task over time, it is one's ability to refresh, re-focus, and renew attention that ensures the successful completion of that task.

Mental Focus

Having an expiration date established for your desired task won't produce results if you are not able to focus in the time period you have identified.

Life optimizer indentifies that there are five levels of mental focus based on the time frame:

- **Lifetime**
- **Yearly**
- **Weekly**
- **Daily**
- **Currently**

How to Focus at All Five Levels

Let's look at the five levels of focus and see how to focus at each of them:

Level 1. Lifetime

Being focused at the lifetime level means that you should have a *purpose* for your life. What is your life purpose? Have you followed it?

Finding your life purpose is perhaps the most difficult thing to do in all five levels, but it is also the most rewarding. It sets the directions of the other levels. If you have this level wrong, you may end up making many wrong decisions in your life.

Here are some things you can do to find your life purpose:

1. ***Find what matters to you-***
   This is the starting point to finding your life purpose. There is one question that can help you find what matters to you:
   "What is the thing that you care so much about that you are willing to do it *for free*?"

2. ***Explore your passions-***
   Don't limit yourself to only one passion. Build your portfolio of passions.

3. ***Find the intersection between your passions and the things that matter to you.***

   The intersections between the things you are passionate about and the things you care about are clear signs of what your life purpose could be.

4. ***Make a mission statement***
   After you have an idea of

what your life purpose is, you should write it in a mission statement. Ideally, it should be a one-liner: ten words or less.

5. ***Keep refining***
   Finding your life purpose is not something you can do in one day or even one year. Just start with what you have and keep refining it. Over time, the direction of your life will be clearer and clearer.

Level 2. Yearly

After dealing with the lifetime level, you should then go down to the yearly level. Here you should have a goal for the year related to your life purpose. Your goal should be both specific and measurable. To ensure that you are focused at the yearly level, you should have only one goal for the year (or two if you must).

One thing to remember is your yearly goal should be related to your life mission. Otherwise, there is a missing link between the lifetime and yearly levels.

Level 3. Weekly

To have focus at weekly level, you should set a goal for the week ahead. What do you want to achieve in the following week to help you achieve your yearly goal?

Level 4. Daily

The next level is daily in which you set your goals for the day. What are the things that you want to achieve today? You can start by setting your Most Important Task (MIT) for the day. Your MIT should be the thing that will make the most difference if you accomplish it today.

Here is a question to help you set your MIT:

"If I can only finish one task today, what will that be?"

You can then set other goals using a variant of the same question:

"If I can only finish one more *task today, what will that be?"*

By asking this question repeatedly you will get a list of the tasks based on priority.

Level 5. Currently

After setting your goals for the day, the next level is the *present*. To get optimum result, you should be focused in whatever you are doing. It means that:

1. You should not multitask
2. You should prevent distractions
3. You should accomplish as much as possible within the time allocated

NOTES

NOTES

Chapter Ten

Accountability Partner

*"What you do in life can be the determining factor of what someone watching you will achieve." -**George Olokun***

WILL YOU SUBMIT TO BEING HELD ACCOUNTABLE EVEN WHEN YOU ARE BEING CHALLENGED?

© by Anna Stevens

There are roughly 7 billion people here on earth and the sad reality is that you will only get an opportunity to meet and interact with a small percentage of those people. When you take a close look at those that you consider your circle of friends or your network, *ask yourself three questions:*

1. **Do they make me better?**

2. **Are they for me, as in have they made my advancement a priority in their life?**

3. Am I accountable to them and them to me?

Anyone that has ever accomplished or achieved something in their life will attest to the fact that they had an accountability partner; a person that kept them from veering too far off track and served as that motivating force when things became somewhat overbearing. An accountability partner is someone who you trust to hold you to the standards that you set for yourself.

An accountability partner does not set goals for you. However, they should be the same type of person you discuss your goals with. They help keep you responsible for the goals you set, and help differentiate between legitimate shortcomings, and the lies we tell ourselves to accept straying off the path of our goals. They should be someone who is not afraid to "*tell you like it is*". There is no room for sugar coating in the realm of personal growth. I've found that one of the benchmarks of a true friend and a person I can count on as an accountability partner is the fact that they can tell me when

I'm failing to reach my potential, see through the lies I'm telling myself, and call me out on it.

Roy Baumeister, in his book, *"Willpower: Rediscovering the Greatest Human Strength"* talks about willpower acting like a muscle that becomes fatigued, and once it is fatigued, becomes less reliable. However, having an accountability partner acts like a "spotter" in the gym. When the weight becomes too difficult to lift by ourselves, we can rely on the strength of an accountability partner to help us make the right decisions and stay on course, even when they are not there.

Julia Eiman, an online blogger clearly articulated seven reasons one should have an accountability partner in an article she shared online. She begins with a popular quote from *Jim Rohn, "When two people come together and share common goals, things will happen."*

Then she goes to outline reasons it's essential to have an accountability partner.

1. They help us **focus** – accountability partners help us keep our eye on the ball

– our goals – and stay on track and not allow us to go off on tangents.

2. They provide **a sounding board** – they are someone to bounce ideas off of and they bring clarity and a fresh perspective to our challenges.

3. They **kick butt** when we need it – they don't accept our excuses and they call us on them.

4. They help us **deal with overwhelming times** – we all feel overwhelmed by all we have to do sometimes. Accountability partners offer suggestions and support to work through the overwhelming times, often suggesting time saving ideas and shortcuts we didn't know about or think about.

5. They help us make good **choices and decisions** – by being good listeners and providing feedback on our thought process, they help us get clarity so we can make better decisions.

6. They are great **cheerleaders** – they encourage and cheer us on and tell us we can achieve our goals. That boosts motivation and feelings of achievement.

7. They remind us to **celebrate our successes** – along the way we need pats on the back and someone to say "good job" when we've done well and created a success. Accountability partners give us virtual hugs, pats on the back and help us appreciate our accomplishments.

Quality Control

"Accountability is the glue that ties commitment to results." ***- Bob Proctor***

Accountability and Responsibility

Most goals are not achieved because you are not held accountable to anyone to achieve them. The second biggest benefit of an accountability partner is that they hold you accountable to reach your goals and monitor your actions to ensure you are on the right path. They act as sounding boards, gatekeepers and test groups all the while asking you where you stand with your plan.

Idea Sharing, Creativity and Brainstorming

Information is one of the most powerful assets a person can posses and having the ability to leverage other people's information is exponentially better. Your accountability partner will come with different experiences, perspectives and ideas that will help you overcome your obstacles and challenges. Having the ability to brainstorm and be creative with another person focused on helping you solve a problem is one of the biggest benefits you will experience from an accountability partner.

Motivational Support

Staying positive and motivated is a big challenge for some especially after the excitement of starting to work on a goal has worn off and the task becomes work. Goals take time, hard work and determination and results often do not come as quickly as one would hope. This can be very frustrating and cause many to become unmotivated. By surrounding yourself with a supportive accountability partner, you will receive positive encouragement no matter how you perform and the active discussions you will participate in will most likely inspire and stimulate you to move forward.

During your search for an accountability partner, keep in mind that the right person should be someone who will challenge, engage and evoke a sense of accomplishment in you. This person should be somebody you admire and are willing to listen to.

The late Steve Jobs, founder of Apple Inc., the world's second-largest information technology company made sure that accountability was at the cornerstone of Apple's management. Not a single meeting without a DRI – direct responsible individual – in charge of a well-defined piece of the puzzle. At the individual level, it's obviously a double edged sword: the person feels really in charge of both success and failure. Jobs had a very profound view on accountability; in one of his interviews he said the following:

> *Do you know how many committees we have at Apple? Zero. We have no committees. We are organized like a startup. We are the biggest startup on the planet. We all meet for three hours once a week and we talk about everything we're doing, the all business. And there is tremendous teamwork at the top of the company which filters down the teamwork through out of the company.*

Jobs encouraged a culture of strict accountability at all level.

NOTES

NOTES

Chapter Eleven

21 Days Magnified

"Every morning we are born again· What we do today is what matters most·" —***Buddha***

WHY WAIT TIL TOMORROW TO START CREATING A NEW HABIT?

It Takes 21 Days to Form a Habit

I'm going to start ______________________________

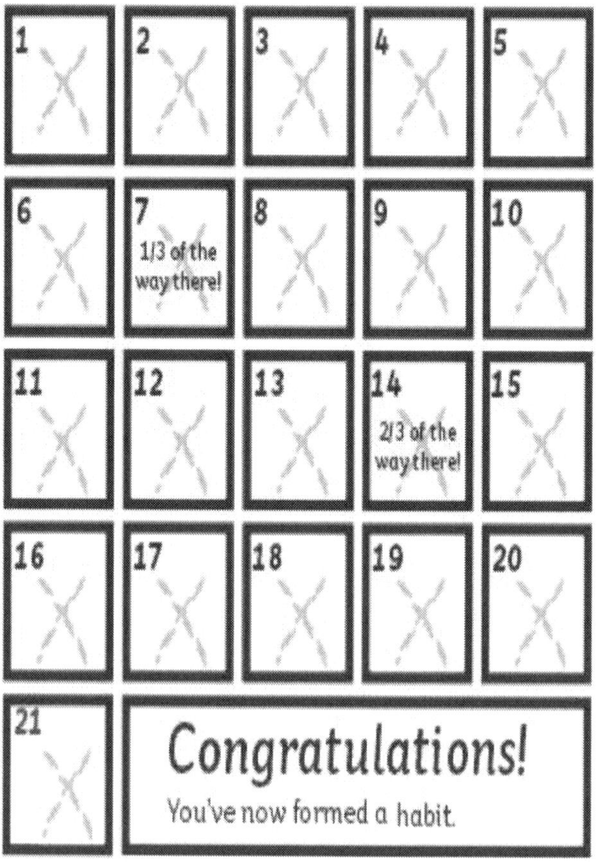

The year was 1960 and a self help book by cosmetic surgeon Dr. Maxwell Maltz, entitled *"Psycho-Cybernetics: A New Way To Get More Living Out Of Life",* centered around the premise that it takes 21 days to form a habit Dr. Martz recommended that humans begin to practice a 21 day cycle of positive behaviors and positive self-affirmations to make their lives better. He wrote *"It takes about 21 days of practice for an old mental image of self to dissolve and a new one to gel".*

Though over the past five decades this idea has become accepted by a vast majority as fact, there are a pocket of people that disagree and feel it takes much longer for your mind to learn a new behavior. I stand firmly with Dr. Maltz and others that believe that each of us can alter our thinking habits with a 21 day cycle. As humans we find ourselves wanting to break our old way of life for a new way, but our biggest challenge is the challenge with our minds.

The mind does not react well with an alteration from regular habits. It is only when you first converse with your mind and form an agreement with your mind that a change must occur, that you can be successful with your new journey towards a better way of life. All thought creation that results from a better way of thinking, becomes solidified by the positive reaffirmation of the mind when the outcome of that new thought creation produces positive results.

If you were to just wake up today and decide that you want to lose ten pounds and for the next 21 days you just relied on your thoughts about losing those ten pounds, you most definitely would not see the results that you desired. You would have to go into that 21 day cycle with a strategy and a plan of action to implement that strategy. The success of your new thought creation around your 21 day cycle that results in a new life behavior, is not predicated on your ability to see immediate results, but the success comes from your ability to maintain your new life behavior long-term.

As you think about what you would rather be doing with your life, it can be very easy to see what it is you would rather be doing, but also very difficult to stop being fearful of the "**WHAT IF?**" This question is a stumbling block; it is your way of combating your minds belief that anything is possible. "What if?" is a paralyzing stumbling block, but it does not have to be permitted to halt your forward progress.

Creating New Life Behaviors

I was reading an article on habit formation and the following was in line with my thought creation around new life behavior. The article stated:

This first phase of habit formation is known as the **"Honeymoon"** and is characterized by the feeling of "this is easy." As all married people will tell you, at some point even the greatest honeymoon must end. The honeymoon phase is usually the result of something inspiring.

For example, a person attends a highly motivational conference, and for the first few days after the conference the individual is making positive changes in his or her life.

The second phase of habit formation is known as the **"THE FIGHT THRU**" and is characterized by the fading of inspiration and reality setting in. A person finds themselves struggling with the positive habit completion and old habits seem to be right around the corner. The key to moving to the third phase of habit formation is to win two or three "fight thru's". This is critical.

To win the fight thru, use the following techniques:

- **RECOGNITION:** Recognition is essential for winning the fight thru. When you have entered the fight through, simply say to yourself, "I have entered the fight thru, and I need to win a few to move past this." Winning each fight thru will make it easier to win the next. Conversely, when you choose to lose a fight thru, you make it easier to lose the next one.

ASK Two Questions:

"How will I feel if I do this?"

"How will I feel if I don't do this?"

- Bring EMOTION into the equation. Let yourself feel the positive in winning the fight thru and the negative in losing.

- **LIFE PROJECTION:** If the above two techniques haven't moved you to action, then imagine in great detail how your life will be in 5 years if you do not begin making changes. Be totally honest with yourself, and allow yourself to feel what life will be like if the changes are not made.

This third phase of habit formation is known as "**SECOND NATURE**". Entering second nature is often described by feelings of "getting in the groove." Once in second nature, the following are three common interruptions that will send a person back to the fight thru:

- **THE DISCOURAGEMENT MONSTER**: An individual allows negative results discourage him or her into thinking, "This isn't working, and there is nothing I can do."
- **DISRUPTIONS:** An individual experiences significant change to his or her current pattern (e.g., vacations, holidays, illness, weekends).
- **SEDUCTION OF SUCCESS:** An individual begins to focus on positive

> results and begins to think, "I'm the special one. I have finally figured out how to have great results with not so great process."

Most people want positive habits to be as easy as brushing their teeth. Being great isn't easy. In fact greatness requires sacrifice. It requires doing things that others won't or can't do. **GREAT HABITS ARE FORMED DAILY**. Truth be told, good habits require consistent commitment. Highly successful people have learned to develop good habits. Make the commitment to make it past the fight thru, no matter how many times you go back to it, to reach new levels of success.

NOTES

NOTES

Focused Sacrifice

"You'll never change your life until you change something you do daily" **-John C. Maxwell**

Meditation is the greatest form of focus that you can learn in your life. It is a practice where you train your mind or induce a mode of consciousness. This also requires a great deal of sacrifice. A sacrifice is the act of giving up something valued for the sake of something else regarded as more important or worthy. How important is your life to you?

ARE

YOU

READY?

Take a moment to list all the things in your life that are important to you that you are willing to sacrifice in order to implement your exit strategy.

About the Author

Bio | George "Mr-Opportunity" Olokun

Personal Life Trainer, Author, Speaker, Thought Leader

Mr-Opportunity's national and international travels have allowed him to speak for several thousand. Since his college days, he has been utilizing his oratorical gift to help transform the lives of everyone. As a world renowned speaker and high potential young entrepreneur he finds himself engaged to opportunity.

Earlier this year, he was named **one of the Top 11 Leading Professional Speakers** in the HBCU community; he's also been featured in the League of Extraordinary Black Men, and has been on MSNBC and C-SPAN.

In 2013, the award winning mentor program by the name of Mentor One, founded by George "Mr-Opportunity" Olokun, is celebrated 10 years of impacting the lives of thousands of high school and college level students.

In 2011, George received the New Leaders Council **National 40 under 40 Leadership Award**, a very prestigious award naming him one of the TOP 40 Progressive Leaders in the Nation.

In 2008, George founded **GDot Empowerment, LLC.** --A Global Enterprise that serves as the parent company of the following entities: GDot Consulting, GDot Publishing Group, and GDot Hospitality Group. From the conference room to the community, George is an extremely passionate individual that loves people and to help others overcome obstacles in their lives.

As an author, thousands have been empowered by his words and publications, which are available in several countries. In 2012, George's second book entitled **"MR-OPPORTUNITY: A Changed Mindset"** was published and has received rave reviews. Two years earlier in 2010, the Amazon Best Seller **"Empowered To Achieve: 50 Keys To Being and Becoming"** was also published.

George served from 2010-2013 as the Founding Chairman & 1st President of the EMERGING 100 of Atlanta; the young professionals auxiliary of the 100 Black Men of Atlanta, Inc., in addition to sitting on the board of directors for two non-profit organization and has held a plethora of other leadership/service roles.

Products

www.Mr-Opportunity.com

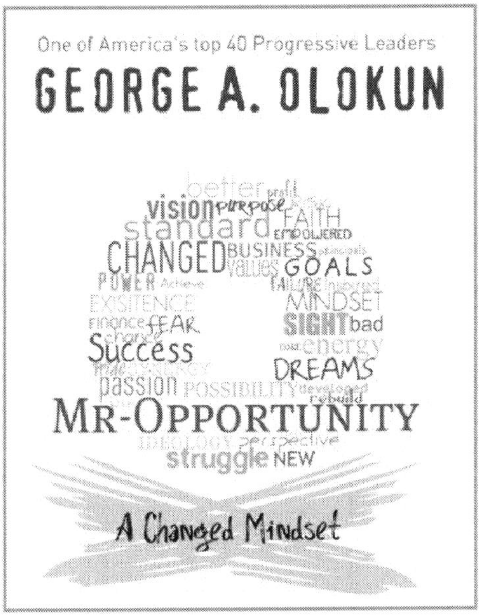

MR-OPPORTUNITY

A Changed Mindset

ISBN 978-0-615-60341-4

Publisher: GDot Publishing Group; (April, 2012)

This Book that will alter the way you see LIFE and redirect your mindset in a direction towards achievement.

This book focuses on how changing your mindset as it relates to life will alter the destination of your life while maximizing on the full potential that's within you.

EMPOWERED TO ACHIEVE

50 Keys To Being And Becoming

ISBN: 978-0-615-38936-3

Publisher: GDot Publishing Group; (July 21, 2010)

The Book is a guide for everyone through life with his 50 Keys of Being and Becoming as the compass. It brings access to Achievement back to the Hands of the reader.

BEST SELLER